THE
ART OF
exile

Bilingual Press/Editorial Bilingüe
Canto Cosas

Series Editor
Francisco Aragón

Publisher
Gary D. Keller

Executive Editor
Karen S. Van Hooft

Associate Editors
Adriana M. Brady
Brian Ellis Cassity
Amy K. Phillips
Linda K. St. George

Address:
Bilingual Press
Hispanic Research Center
Arizona State University
PO Box 875303
Tempe, Arizona 85287-5303
(480) 965-3867

To Cristina:
a book of poems
from a small
country,
Archila

Georgetown University
_3/20/12_

THE
ART OF
exile

WILLIAM ARCHILA

William Archila

Bilingual Press/Editorial Bilingüe

Tempe, Arizona

Library of Congress Cataloging-in-Publication Data

Archila, William.
    The art of exile / William Archila.
        p. cm.
    ISBN 978-1-931010-52-8 (pbk. : alk. paper)
    1. El Salvador—Poetry. I. Title.

    PR9298.9.A17A89 2008
    811'.6—dc22

                                                    2008024784

PRINTED IN THE UNITED STATES OF AMERICA

Front cover art: Back View *(2005) by Ramón Ramírez*

Cover and interior design by Bill Greaves

This publication is supported in part by an award from The National Endowment for the Arts.

NATIONAL
ENDOWMENT
FOR THE ARTS

Canto Cosas

Funded in part by grants from the National Endowment for the Arts and the Arizona Commission on the Arts, this new series is designed to give further exposure to Latina and Latino poets who have achieved a significant level of critical recognition through individual chapbooks and publication in periodicals or anthologies or both, but who have not necessarily had their own books of poetry published. Under the watchful eye of series editor, poet, and small press publisher Francisco Aragón, the books in Canto Cosas aim to reflect the aesthetic diversity in American poetry. There are no restrictions on ethnicity, nationality, philosophy, ideology, or language; we will simply continue our commitment to producing high-quality poetry. The books in this series will also feature introductions by more established voices in the field.

Language is the only homeland.

—Czeslaw Milosz

Contents

Foreword: *Where the Heart Is,* Yusef Komunyakaa   xi

I

Radio   3

The decade the country became known throughout the world   6

Latest News   8

Ten   10

Duke Ellington, Santa Ana, El Salvador, 1974   12

biography of a country   14

Northbound   15

From the black fields   16

By the Highway   18

1978   19

This Earth   21

II

Immigration Blues, 1980   25

Two o'clock in the morning   27

Self-Portrait with Crow   28

Bird   29

A Dying Sun   31

Drinking Beer in East L.A.   33

This is for Henry   34

Foreign Language   37

Whitman   39

At Minton's   41

Late December   43

Palm Tree   45

Guayaberas   47

The Gift   49

On first listening to Coltrane   51

Pilgrimage   53

Small Country   55

III

After Ashes   59

IV

The Art of Exile   67

Rattle   69

Roque   70

Two-bass lines   72

Bicycle   74

Bury This Pig   76

Tunnel   78

Acknowledgments   79

Where the Heart Is

Yusef Komunyakaa

I met William Archila during the summer of 2005, at the Breadloaf Writer's Conference, and from the onset I was truly impressed by his quiet demeanor and fire-tinged poetry. He already possessed a facility for assaying the sonorities of a multilayered world—lived and imagined. Indeed, here was a voice that seemed old and young, a singer of naked praise and lamentation, a truth seeker and truth teller, a poet who resided with certitude and a sense of grace, uniquely within his own skin, without any bravado or grandstanding. In his best poems, a quiet certainty lived alongside a natural surrealism. Early on, there was already something (how does one explain it, or should one even attempt to explain it?) in a poem by Archila, indebted to a strangeness that seemed matter-of-fact, and an almost casual gravity and buoyancy were intricately woven into that which approximated everyday life. Nothing felt contrived or ornamental in a poem by this fine young poet; this fact kept me returning to his work again and again.

Now, a few years later, sitting here in New York City with *The Art of Exile*, I am reminded of what truly struck a nerve in me when I first read William Archila's poetry: I believe the authenticity in this voice. This is a voice of a witness. If not through first-hand experience, then at least through the careful, needful capture of those familial voices that have direct ownership of the pain and moments of celebration that humanize these lyrical pages. A poet of the heart and head, of the personal and public, at times William Archila poignant poems make me hear and feel an echo of Pablo Neruda and Cesar Vallejo. Even when the imagination navigates the subconscious, this young poet's unearthed imagery is believable, as is clearly depicted in a poem such as "Self-Portrait with Crow":

As I punch the time-clock, I know
men will be gunned down at dawn
in a distant continent, someone
will dart into a café with a bomb nestled

in the belly, by the roadside a woman
will moan over the body of a man,
shrunken, stretched on the earth, that God
will finger the forehead of a dying country,

all of it funneled through the news on TV.
But tonight, instead of tuning in, I'm going to kneel
beside the window, recognize myself
in the croak of the crow, high above the black tree

of winter, claws hooked and rough, wings swept
back and hunched, face masked with exhaust.
I'm going to try, even if I fail, to see myself whole,
complete in the cry, in the beak of the crow.

There are numerous conjured masks and rituals in *The Art of Exile;*
however, they never serve as avenues of escape, but as mechanisms of con-
frontation, paths toward wholeness, always shying away from any kind of
diminishment. And, in that sense, even when the speakers are attempting
to traverse the psyche and bowels of the underworld, Archila's imagery and
language negotiate moments of healing.

Here's a master of observation. Nothing escapes Archila's astute eye; his
scrutiny seems to owe everything to a practiced seeing, a seeing informed
by the elemental: land, water, animal, human and spiritual beings. Old gods
seem to live under the eyelids of this seer who has been fully initiated by
birth and rendered a facility for gifted insight. Music is central to Archila's
vision—not for the sake of entertainment, but a music that lights a path back
to the land and its earthy surety. Also, it is a music that cross borders in flesh

and spirit, as the speaker in "Duke Ellington, Santa Ana, El Salvador, 1974"
so aptly exacts in the poem's final two stanzas:

> He could be my grandfather,
> black boy from Chalatenango—
> indigo-blue family
> from the Caribbean through Honduras.
> He could be the one to write
> a tone parallel to Sonsonate,
> a trombone to roll to the wheels
> of a cart, the wrinkled man,
> toothless, pulling his corn.
>
> More than a Congo drum in a cabaret,
> more than a top hat and tails before a piano,
> I want him to come back,
> his orchestra to pound the doors
> of a ballroom by the side of a lake.
> I want the cracked paint to peel off the walls,
> lights to go dim, floors to disappear,
> a trumpet to growl,
> my country to listen.

Again, this poet's work seeks wholeness. Attempting to bridge race and
class, some of Archila's poems bring characters and people together in a space
that is more than imaginary. In "Small Country," when the speaker says "I
know how to follow great avenues, / the stump of a cigarette between my
teeth unlit" I believe him, that he's standing on solid ground—within and
outside of metaphor.

And, yes, there's another abiding force in Archila's poetry. His playful
wit is addictive. Some of the poems in *The Art of Exile* are balanced with a
signifying akin to that found in seasoned blues singers and masters of the
jailhouse toast. He knows how to intermix pain and laughter, as if one were

the other. In that sense, a satirical sobriety pulses at the center of each poem, as is the case illustrated in "Drinking Beer in East, L.A.":

> This is how he always wanted to remember himself:
> leaning against the green Impala, something brown and juicy,
> like Willie Bobo blowing out of the speakers,
>
> sweat steaming down the eyebrows, his buddies
> hanging out like lions in the heat, spread out over the hood,
> watching the sun melt the asphalt,
>
> the boulevard glowing with a line of low riders, puffing,
> bouncing all the way down to the bald,
> yellow mountains, where the outline of smog thickens
> and the rickety houses wait for a can full of rain.
>
> He would hook the bottle opener to the neck,
> pop the cap off—a geyser of foam—a shot
> for the lady tattooed on his back, his throat
> ready for the long, cool rush of a false god.

William Archila's *The Art of Exile* shows the poet's genius, his work as a tableau for the larger community of everyday concerns and imagistic inquiry. I believe in his poetry, spirit and heart.

I

Radio

"Puedo escribir los versos más tristes esta noche.
Escribir, por ejemplo, 'La noche está estrellada. . . .' "

That was Neruda through a small plastic portable,
blue with white knobs, when I was ten
and mother woke me to listen

by the red needle of the dial, its window
throwing a half-yellow light in the bedroom,

his voice reaching the darkest corner
of the house, words full of rain, ancient,

from a foreign planet, lapping at my bedside,
fat waves rocking against a boat, prow

reaping through the waters, a sound
like the whoosh of pine trees bending.

The set was big enough for the rusted gun
mother hid inside, right above the batteries,

a piece ready to target soldiers
on rooftops, camouflaging the dawn,

or the men of tattered clothes, tired eyes,
rifles in their hands, running down
coffee mountain to palace wall.

The poems kept coming, calmed,
relaxed, as if walking back
from a lake, the rise and fall

of waves closing over each other,
ignorant of my father on the phone,
calling long distance from Los Angeles,

his voice, a buzz and a click, clipped
by the blackouts of a tiny country.

Who knows what kept
my father in the north? Perhaps
it was the city lights of a woman,

long snouts of avenues
clutching their tongues, unrolling
the drunken dollar flat on his hand.

Perhaps it was the vertebrae of broken bodies
caught in the gutter. Who knows

if he knew that wind flew
around our house, howling like a dog?

That his wife came to bed
as if rejected by the moon once again,

radio in the crook of her arm
tuned to the dark shade of pines,
"lento juego de luces, campana solitaria."

I lay in bed, my mother's breath lost
deep in the absence of her husband—my ears
wide open to darkness,

listening to the lines of a faint voice
crackle and glow, a radio that enters evening
like a boatman standing in the mist,

feeling waves roll underneath, pulling me
through the slow nights of a small war.

The decade the country became known throughout the world

The ground cracked
like the rough pit of a peach
and snapped in two.
The sun behind the mountains
turned into an olive-green glow.

To niña Gloria this was home.
She continued to sell her bowl of lemons,
rubbing a cold, thin silver Christ
pocketed in her apron. Others
like Lito and Marvin played
soldiers in the ruins of a school,
running around mounds of bricks,
       shooting chickens and pigs.

No one knows exactly how
a light film of ash appeared
on everyone's eyelids
       early in the morning
or how trout and mackerel plunged from the sky,
twitched, leaped through the streets.

Some say the skin of trees
felt like old newspaper, dry and yellow.
Others believe the soapsuds
washed aside in rivers
began to rise in their milk.

One Monday morning, a rain fell
and the cemetery washed into the city.
Bones began to knock

and knock at our doors.
Streets became muddy rivers
waiting for bodies to drop
            among piles of dead fish.

In a year, everyone stabbed flowers on a grave.

This explains why women thought
and moved like lizards under stones,
why men heard bees buzzing inside their skulls,
why dogs lost their sense of smell
sniffing piles of rubble to get back home.

In a few years, no one cared
about turtles banging their heads against rocks,
bulls with their sad, busted eyes,
parrots that kept diving into creeks,
the dark swelling of the open ground
            or at night a knife
                  stained the kitchen cloth.

Instead, niña Gloria swept the ground,
the broom licking her feet at each stroke.

At the bus station, Marvin shined
military boots,
            twenty-five cents a pair,
reduced his words to a spit, a splutter
of broken sentences
            on shoe polish, leather.

In the evenings, he counted coins
he'd tossed in a jar, then walked home,
one step closer to the cracked bone
clenched in the yellow jaw of a dog.

Latest News

At work, no one has seen him or his taxi.
Newspapers read, "Juan Márquez Missing:
Any sighting, please contact family."

A few months ago, police led a trail
to graves: some broken bones,
the kind you find in times of war.

In Nicaragua, they remember him,
poet so blue and modern like Darío,
almost a song of swans about to break.

Honduras spoke of him naked, hairless,
barefoot, tobacco skin without toenails
or ears, a man of ants and stray dogs.

Two weeks ago, a boy found a body
dark as eggplant. His wife, worn and rumpled,
could not recognize the blown-out face.

My mother thinks he's deep in the ground,
sleeping with torn clothes, thick,
dank roots spreading over his limbs.

The rumor goes at night in smoky bars
he met Jesus of Nazareth, a red lightbulb
flickering on and off in the corner.

Today I heard he's a bus driver
in L.A., circling long avenues,
parks, the same hotel signs, traffic

lights, the rain that falls at night.
Around ten, a rumor goes he gets lost
in a downtown dive, drinks his shot of gin.

Don Chamba, a shoe shiner from Santa Ana,
gave me the final word the other day.
"To me," he says, "those stories don't mean shit.

By now, after all those small deaths,
he has to be a soiled shoe, a worn-out tire,
aflame, smoking by an empty highway."

Ten

That summer, with sticky fingers
I learned to read coins, count a dime
for bread, a quarter for eggs,
sold Coca-Colas over the counter.

I stood, slapping at flies buzzing
over plums, melons and mangos.
The sun, old copper in the palms
of my hands, trickled drops of sweat,

then rills of brown muddy waters
down my ankles, green rubber sandals.
Across the street, girls sweet
in their dresses sat on the curb,

steam rising from their shoulders,
admiring the boys shirtless at soccer.
They had a gift for the game,
they thought with their feet,

slept every night with a plastic
ball still dusty from the streets.
I joined them, left behind
fruits and flies, swished along

the field, dribbling passes
back and forth, cursing the heat
glued to our skin, then a tic-
tac-toe, the ball spinning

in the air, until it curved
mid-flight, flew right into the post.
And we began again, down
the sideline, cutting the defense.

For a moment, the greats of Europe
bowed their heads as a sign of respect.
Those evenings, the red sun
clumped down the coffee mountains.

I continued to sell Coca-Colas.
Fifty for cheese, the sticky coins
in the palms of my hands, the growing degrees
of summer spiraling up from my feet.

Duke Ellington, Santa Ana, El Salvador, 1974

He paces the cool, dusty classroom,
hands in his pockets, rows of chairs,
sixth-grade children looking straight
at him, watching his big-band walk.

At the blackboard, he turns
and breaks the silence.
"Instead of crossing an Oriental garden,
picture a desert under a devil sun."

He snaps his fingers two plus one
as if to say one more time.
We shout back a demented version of *Caravan*,
crashing cymbals, drums, bent horns—
muffled rhythms from a line of saxophones.

Edwin Martínez gets on his feet, leans over
the music stand and tortures the trumpet,
pouring all his memories of Egypt from history class.
Douglas Díaz slaps the bongos
exactly the same way he beats on
cans of coffee and milk at home.

Señor Ellington claps his hands along,
dancing a two-step blues, stomping
in the center of everyone like a traffic cop
conducting a busy city street.
Before break he will tell us
stories of a smoky blue spot
called the Cotton Club.

We will learn all the Harlem rhapsodies
from the Latin Quarter up to 125th Street.
He will swing the piano keys, a syncopated phrase
and we will listen: no need to study war no more.

He could be my grandfather,
black boy from Chalatenango—
indigo-blue family
from the Caribbean through Honduras.
He could be the one to write
a tone parallel to Sonsonate,
a trombone to roll to the wheels
of a cart, the wrinkled man,
toothless, pulling his corn.

More than a Congo drum in a cabaret,
more than a top hat and tails before a piano,
I want him to come back,
his orchestra to pound the doors
of a ballroom by the side of a lake.
I want the cracked paint to peel off the walls,
lights to go dim, floors to disappear,
a trumpet to growl,
my country to listen.

biography of a country

Mid-continent, the earth opens like a cut.
Beneath the stained chalice, a priest in black gets shot.
Soldiers in green climb rooftops like iguanas after dark.

Down the road, an oxcart with sacks of coffee creaks.
Heavy rain falls through lemon leaves, grasshoppers.
The earth opens up like a cut.

Black mud flows down mountains, along cobblestones,
clings to our shoes, hardens to clay almost gray.
Soldiers with white faces climb like iguanas at night,

their grip on rifles twisted into knots of blue veins.
Above, the thup-thup of helicopters breaks the sky.
In this country, the earth opens like a cut.

The lightbulb dims on pale yellow windows,
thin bodies with red eyes who watch doors,
soldiers who climb like iguanas at night.

Think of the dead eating wet dirt,
the dead who have come back to claim their shoes
in a country where the earth opens up like a cut,
soldiers climb and climb like iguanas after dark.

Northbound

Empty, outside Cuzcatlán,
the highway tears through
coffee fields like a knife,
roadside weeds yellow and green.
The soldiers are gone,

leaving two bodies sprawled
face down, side by side in a ditch,
a reflection in the vulture's eye.

Out here, the sky's so blue
you could grab it with your hand,
sunlight splayed across the clouds,
a hymn of skies trailing
a crater black with ash.

On the ground, a heap of ants tear away
the splintered shell of a cockroach
left and right. They bury themselves
in the hole. I leave them there
in the claw of God.

From the black fields

He couldn't bear all those open graves,
        black mud, hyacinths falling apart,
all those coffins that broke

his sleep, their dead fists cold as rocks.
        That's why he leaves the fields
where he cut cane

at the first flush of dawn,
        military men, their M-16s
strapped across their backs, helmets

across their eyes. They stood
        beside him as he cut
the land into plots,

pale and dry, plowed
        and plowed for a fistful of dimes,
the wooden shack for a bar

where Corporal Martínez got knifed,
        the dagger stabbed
in the back, truckloads of peasants

carted away to the barracks,
        tires tracking the ground.
The trees darken by the roadside

as he hurries past brick houses,
        tin flats, the long path of earth that stretches
in front of him, the miles

between him and his boy,
             standing in a soccer field
more dirt than yellow grass, his wife sound asleep

on a bed of palms, bits of dresses and rags.
             Soil, pebbles clump together,
stick in the hollows of his soles, dust

thick in the lines of his palms.
             From the black fields
the branches stick out their arms.

By the Highway

The sun, a small bowl
in the morning sky
finds a slumped body
on dirt ground. Peasant

hands, two knots of fists
swollen and stiff, deep
dark creases like two
strong Nicaraguan

cigars, laid open
nailed with dust. The eyes,
two burnt-out votives
or empty jail cells,

tell the chronicles
of last night: rifle
butts that cracked open
a body, tattered,

twisted, broken frame
of bones. Luis is dead.
Dead without his shoes.
Nothing in my hands

can bring him back to
walk this earth, lost in
the pale golden rows
of cornstalk and sun.

1978

The police chased Chico at least twice a week.
He ran barefoot along gritty, unpaved streets.

None of us knew why these officers
in green, billy clubs raised in the air, chased

this thin fifteen-year-old down the alleyways.
At school, none of us saw him sneak in late,

His blue uniform faded, books fastened
with a belt buckle thrown over the shoulder.

I loved the way he stood
next to the blackboard, chalk in hand,

teaching us how to step across
a soccer field, zigzag right through defenders,

how to rock the ball to sleep on our heads, knees.
One afternoon, he nailed the ball straight

into the net. We all jumped, shouted,
"What a lovely goal!" Even the goalkeeper

got off the ground to shake his hand.
That year, air smelled of gunpowder

in Nicaragua. Prisoners in Argentina
were beaten, pushed from airplanes

into the wrinkled waters of the Atlantic sea.
All of us watched the World Cup

on a black-and-white TV, bits of newspaper scattered
like rainfall across the stadium. All of us

continued to kick that mother of a plastic ball
without meeting Pelé, without knowing

the dusty smells of a university classroom.
"Who is Shakespeare? Don Quixote?"

In prison, on a piss-stained wall,
with a piece of soap in hand, Chico

drew a Z, taught his mates how to dribble
across the grass, slide the ball

all the way down the side wings,
how to arc the ball to the corner net,

and break from your man.
No one spoke. No one breathed

when Chico entered the field, galloped
with the police at his heels.

This Earth

Every morning, I think about the war,
smell of gasoline and burning buses,
how the dead fall into our beds,
wither into the earth.

When Monseñor Romero died, my mother said,
"One thousand Romeros now raise their arms."
That year newspapers displayed coffins
lined up in college auditoriums.

TV news played images of planes
like knives flying through neighborhoods.
I watched the sun crawl out of the mountains
across a small Vietnam.

Days turned the pages of a textbook.
Memo and I sat together in our uniforms,
all showered and combed, shoes shined,
handkerchiefs folded in our back pockets.

We memorized countries, studied oceans,
this globe, a plastic soccer ball
we kicked in the streets with unknown children,
hot soil burning the bottoms of our feet.

"If death should come knocking on my door,
tell him to come back tomorrow," Memo always joked.
"I still haven't touched Patty in the restroom."
He never laid a hand on her.

The afternoon she pressed her body into mine,
a fisherman brought him home in an orange

plastic bag: a leg, an arm, one brown shoe still on.
He was found by the side of a lake.

After the burial, everyone slept with the light on.
No sounds in the street, but the whistle of a blue cricket.
I thought of him barefoot, darkening the ground,
the wings of black birds covering his body.

So many months have gone by, so many buried
under stones, their once stiffened bodies now dust.
Somewhere in the mist, I know the earth,
cold and damp with rain, belongs to them.

At dusk, when the sun hides
behind the mountains, I watch the neighbors,
all soiled, figures almost baked in clay,
come back from the greasy stacks of factories.

This could be Memo,
trudging across a charred city,
crumbling into the streets, hungry
for a plate of chicken and beans, maybe beer.

Night arrives. There's no one in the street now,
only the cricket deep in the alley.
I pull the string from the lightbulb,
remember my geography book,

the bombed-out walls of my school,
neighbors closing doors, nailing their eyes shut,
Memo under my feet, how I love the smell of wet dirt,
how I will cup my hands, carry this earth in my pockets.

II

Immigration Blues, 1980

Hiding in a cloud of cigarette smoke,
black as a crow, I walk streets
long and dark, cracked,
open like the carcass of a dead cat.

Every corner, a tattered palm tree
pokes at the moon. Steam rises
out of four circles in a pothole.
I'm a war away from home,

away from that tiny scratch
on a boy's knee, that crumbled corner
of earth where death rattles
its brown paper bag of bones.

I'm a man with black hair, raw accent,
Spanish syllables caught in my throat,
words in English locked in a dictionary,
a foreigner everywhere I go.

Under the freeway overpass,
cars driving around groan,
their lungs rusting with smog.
I think of torn bodies, cramped,

unburied in a ditch, covered
in weeds or dust. They become items
for the evening news, documents
from another small-foot country,

another Lebanon, a mile from God.
They come to me in letters,
mid-sentence, blue ink that stains
and glows on my fingers. I'm lost

among buildings downtown,
pronouncing the sound of their names
in the hollow roof of my mouth,
spelling them over

and over again, till they mean
nothing, nothing at all.

My country falls on me like a hammer.

Two o'clock in the morning

They groan about Christ, his foot slapped
on their skulls, his memory clear
like their dead lost in the pale grass,
their graves are many and unmarked.

They stay for days, too many weeks,
eating beans and fried chicken necks,
drinking frosted beers topped with foam.
They come from countries far and small.

They learn to mop from sun to sun,
breed fowl and nurse the boss's child,
remember the green coast back home,
something sharp rusting on their tongues.

They knock with busted knuckles, step
inside with tattered coats, shoes torn,
come from graves far and small,
unmarked. They wait at the bus stop.

Self-Portrait with Crow

As I punch the time-clock, I know
men will be gunned down at dawn
in a distant continent, someone
will dart into a café with a bomb nestled

in the belly, by the roadside a woman
will moan over the body of a man,
shrunken, stretched on the earth, that God
will finger the forehead of a dying country,

all of it funneled through the news on TV.
But tonight, instead of tuning in, I'm going to kneel
beside the window, recognize myself
in the croak of the crow, high above the black tree

of winter, claws hooked and rough, wings swept
back and hunched, face masked with exhaust.
I'm going to try, even if I fail, to see myself whole,
complete in the cry, in the beak of the crow.

Bird

On the bus to Lincoln Heights,
I face a boy with a green backpack,
a geography book open on his lap, fingers
stroking the veins of a map,
lips moving in rhythm,
maybe a poem in Spanish, a prayer
so simple and slow I could recognize
every word from my childhood.

As a boy I imagined that before Christ
and the rusty nails, before Columbus,
the gilded cross, Central America
must have been a quetzal, a young bird
with green wings, long tails,
flying over lakes, cluster of volcanoes.

Look at the fold out map
from *National Geographic*.
You can see its beak
northwest of Guatemala.
Legs stretch out into Panama,
its blue back down Honduras and Nicaragua.

Study the topography
and the land rises out of the water,
names of rivers, roads sprawled
over the graphs. You can follow the train
on rails of night, around coffee mountains,
through dark fields of corn, cane,
along rooftops burned red,
away from the soft lights of a brick house.

The full sun breaks on the stairs,
catches the muzzle of a shotgun,
black ball piercing a bird
that drops in a puddle, wrecked.
A light rain falls. You can imagine
that before insects, before the slow crumble
of bones, its legs stretch out, back curves,
beak rises as though in flight.
Search graves and ruins,
dark branches of palm trees
swallowing pyramids—fragments of ancient stones.

I go back to the boy, black hair,
long brown nose, silver cross around his neck,
book closed, zipped in his backpack.
He holds a sugarcane stick,
stripping the peel with his teeth. We sit
for another minute or two
while the great city cranks ahead.

At Broadway and Daily, he gets off,
before I lose him from the yellow window of my seat,
he runs through a crowd of women and men
coming home from work, past the mailbox,
around the corner store, arms spread apart,
chest forward.

He had the same gaze that glides
over the ocean, same bearing of a flight
over a sailing ship breaking waves,
a lookout manning a crow's nest.
For miles, you can hear a voice calling out,
"Bird! Land at first sight."

A Dying Sun

As the west fades into evening, a painter captures
the flush of a pre-Columbian sun, dying
against buildings downtown,
windows bathed in an orange flood.

He attempts to catch the glow every day
until it is a delicate tint of blue,
and the oil paints run out, his fingers exhausted,
paintings shelved in a garage.

If the light reaches my father,
he will not recognize the sun
with pre-Columbian tattoos, disk
growing old and brown,

hallowed and coined
above the city. My father
will shade his eyes from the light
for he's too busy cutting fabric

in a tin-can shack for a hotel in Hawaii,
unrolling ply after ply, pattern
of uniforms laid flat, cutting machine's
fierce blade slashing

around pockets and back.
Then tying the bundles again,
only to trek, shoulder
another roll of dacron and cotton,

switching weight from knee
to busted knee,
                    cartilage gone thin
and yellow, old bones close to dust,
lint overwhelming his lungs.

By evening, he'll be ready for the couch,
TV, the glare of moving pictures
that will put him to sleep,
his body snoring the cold in and out.

He will not see the geometry of pyramids
busting out of the asphalt, how soon
we forget the red clay of men
scooped out of the earth, the gods

who spit down upon them.

Drinking Beer in East L.A.

This is how he always wanted to remember himself:
leaning against the green Impala, something brown and juicy,
like Willie Bobo blowing out of the speakers,

sweat steaming down the eyebrows, his buddies
hanging out like lions in the heat, spread out over the hood,
watching the sun melt the asphalt,

the boulevard glowing with a line of low riders, puffing,
bouncing all the way down to the bald,
yellow mountains, where the outline of smog thickens
and the rickety houses wait for a can full of rain.

He would hook the bottle opener to the neck,
pop the cap off—a geyser of foam—a shot
for the lady tattooed on his back, his throat
ready for the long, cool rush of a false god.

This is for Henry

It always starts here,
over the chain-linked fence
        with crooked fingers,

leather shoes, running
across the railroad tracks,

        no sound but a gasp
for breath, our white shirts flapping
like flags, cops in black behind.

Sometimes, it's you kneeling
at the corner of the liquor store, handcuffed,
        baton blow
to your back, flopping
to the ground, a grunt
        of flesh and bone,
your golden tooth shining.

This is what I remember
when I drive through east L.A., the boys leaning
        against the wall, rising above trash
            cans, beer bottles,

baggy pants and black
shades, long white shirts
        with two clown faces
above the left breast: one laughing,
        the other crying.

I think
we were fifteen
when we worked in the dark kitchen,
        restaurant heat
            of vegetables and spices,
bags of rice, boxed beer from China.

During breaks, you stood in the alley,
        your shirt over the shoulder
like a towel, whistling
at the girls strolling

their short skirts, exposing
        the lighter skin
            of their bodies.

Around midnight, after carrying
        the last crate of dishes, we untied
our wet aprons.

        I sat across from you
munching on bread, Italian sausages,
swigging on a bottle of wine,
your talk thick as honey—
            marijuana visions of North
            America: blonde girls and their bikinis,
            low riders at night, you in a zoot suit
                and Bruce Lee.

Fifteen years will pass
before I think of you again,
deportation to a village
        between cane fields at dusk,

your disappearance between the Eucharist
and the clang of the bell
early Sunday morning.

I'm a teacher now,
fingers of chalk, papers piled around me.
Sometimes, in the dark eyes
of students, you appear,
your white shirt, shiny shoes,

your back slouched
at the board, cracking the English grammar.

On the street corner, a boy
flashes a hand sign

and it all starts again,
climbing over the fence, running through east L.A.

Foreign Language

One in the morning, rain almost black
falls hard on the bay, waters breathing,

flapping against the dock; the moon
scales the cityscape. I hunch

beneath the yellow desk lamp
with my pencil, sharp as a needle,

stitching this monster of language. English,
a Viking ship tearing the waves

of some southern sea, hieroglyphs engraved
on stones green with moss, sounds locked

in lines, each single word a bag of bones,
each sentence a cluster of characters

I must animate, black marks
that don't roll from my tongue, don't fit

under my skin. Words collapse,
won't make a sound or a dead mariner's shoe.

I scribble roots of verbs, watch
long blades of grass push through the earth.

The sea enters the room. A great fang
or tusk plunges deeper into the ocean,

currents of cold water, lines, loops and dots
lose themselves in the sea of night,

spiral down the drain, down to the shipwreck,
full of cold clammy shoes, dead cables.

The rain has stopped. I sit, stuttering
the open pages of *Moby Dick*,

the baroque rolling tongue of my birth.
Soon the moon will sink into black waters.

Olive-green fish, slick and long, will surface at doorsteps,
their tails slapping the floor, gills opening.

Whitman

For evening walks in the city, I carry a book in my pocket
—dusty pages of bark set out in the sun.

The avenues run with the traffic grind, clang of cable cars
pulling downtown, smoke scattered everywhere.

The boy at the newsstand packs to go home; he's dog-tired
from shouting all day into the air, "He was seen by the waters."

Shoe-shine boy sitting next to him folds his newspaper
like a map, tells me, "It's all true."

From the moon-café, a piano rolls out into the street,
finger bones of a black man hover over the keys.

At the end of the street, atop the entrance of a black skyscraper,
a neon sign flickers in green: What is the grass?

On the stained walls of an alley, someone has painted
with long, red strokes, thick letters, "He was here."

What if all this is true? Who is the old man with a white beard
sitting on the bench, smoking a cigar?

What if the mechanics, firemen, ferryboat pilots,
workers of the streets, all knew him?

On blue-cold streets, we meet strangers,
turn our eyes away into the smoke or passing cars.

We spend hours drawn out by the ticking clock,
living inside our skin, away from words raised in sunlight,

away from the tapping sound of heat, handful clap of dirt,
between curled fingers, a snap of leaves.

But I still see him, his echo deepening in the shade, leaves blue,
wet with rain. I hear him in the woman in rags,

she's pushing a cart, butcher sharpening knives, farmer
picking grapes, his brown arched back rising like a tired sun.

You can't tell me the immigrant reciting lines on the bus,
standing next to the driver, doesn't have his voice of soil, roots.

Night stretches over rooftops. The machinery has stopped.
The multitude goes home, but it's a silent walk.

At Minton's

Monk. I saw him walk
the plot of dead earth,
ground churning

under his toes,
his coat flapped open
to the black slap

of the cold. I saw him
lose himself in the ear
of a saxophone,

piano keys
tucked in dust, blue
bass-tone of night. My eyes

locked down on his hands
wrinkled into the streets
of a city map,

headlights of cars
mumbling up and down
the flat boulevards,

machinery
of cable cars
blinking, crisscrossing

under the half-moons
of his fingernails,
yellow and cracked,

on the wet dirt
in the pockets
of his mouth. There

I came back many nights
to hear him play
the architecture

of the rain, rhythm
of strange colored lights
and their geometry,

tap, hands flat, the brass
and topography
of the metropolis.

Late December

Cold with the wet foliage of wind,
      dappled leaves swollen
under my feet, I enter the rail
of words, bruised buildings arching above.

Each step, someone staggers behind,
leather shoes scraping along the street.
      I turn once, twice. There's no one
only car grease gleaming. I pause,

suddenly the smell of earth
touches my shoulder—dried humus,
      soil entangled in roots. It's you, Lico,
in a black suit and white shirt,
      face of a moon, dark like a dog,

your torn shoes still dusty from the road
      where you fell without a vigil
or gypsies strumming guitars.

This is the bell of the hour,
the dead yellow husk of corn.
      This is the wreckage of insects
      that drowns in the inkwell,
          the rooster of rooftops
      choking down its philosophers.

I often think of you
sitting on rocks by a fire
      under the Brooklyn Bridge

talking about the Spain of the Arabs,
      a band of black men moaning
            the spiral blues of a train.

I want to stay here, standing in front of you,
exchanging the dirt in our pockets,
      songs we carry from our countries,

words we lack
      to cut a hole in the cornfield,
bury the women and men
      with a silver spoon,
childhood of balconies,
          moons and clocks we have lost.

Palm Tree

Far from the ocean crunching at rocks,
black sand drenched in salt water,

the palm tree in L.A. sways nightly,
gray and bruised as the freeways,
roots tangled in rusty pipelines.

The barefoot boys spent their days
         climbing palm trees

on the coastline of Sonsonate,

bottoms of their feet slapped tight
against shaggy trunks, machete in hand,
sun streaking through the fronds,

a coconut always fell with a thump.

The heat, thick as oil, stretched out
                   the slow hours of the sea;

their feet trudged across sand,
                eyes drowned in sweat,
         oval husks swinging from their hands.

The shore turned
to the chopped muck of their lives,
the fish smell
         they carry in their lungs,

language of hooks and bait,
measured stroke of an oar,

their hands, two stripped twigs,
pulling weeds out of a net,
below the seagulls,
                    their boats moving.

It's winter in L.A.,
no rain, just a lashing wind.

I read Martí's *Simple Verses*,
the four opening lines, his love
for the palm grove.

All I want is to collapse
among the lines, pierce my fingers
into the strand, find the first tight,
twisted root, the evergreen
            featherlike leaves gathered at the crown.

Guayaberas

In my boyhood, all the men

wore them, a light body shirt
with pleats running down the breast,
two top pockets for pens, notepads,

two bottom ones for keys or loose change,
each sewn with a button

in the middle of the pouch,
a complement tailored to the slit
at the side of the hip. If you look

at photographs in family albums,
men stand against palm trees,

their short-sleeved guayaberas
caught in sunlight, their Panama hats
tipped to the sky. There's a black and white

of my father, stumbling along fields
of cane, head full of rum,

mouth in an O, probably
singing a bolero of Old San Juan.
On days like these, the sun burned

like an onion in oil. Women hung
guayaberas on windows to dry.

Shirtless, men picked up their barefoot babies
off the floor, held them against their bellies
as if talking to a god. Even my school uniform

was a blue guayabera, but nothing
like my father's favorite: white,
long-sleeved, above the left breast

a tiny pocket, perfectly slender for a cigar,
arabesque designs vertically stretched.

When the evening breeze lulled
from tree to tree, he serenaded

my mother, guitars and tongues of rum
below her balcony; the trio strumming,
plucking till one in the morning.

I don't know what came first,
war or years of exile,
but everyone—shakers of maracas, cutters

of cane, rollers of tobacco—stopped wearing them,
hung them back in the closet, waiting

for their children to grow,
an arc of parrots to fly across the sky
at five in the evening. In another country,

fathers in their silver hair sit
on their porches, their sons, now men,

hold babies in the air, guayaberas nicely pressed.

The Gift

I always wanted to truck Coca-Cola bottles to villages
made of dirt, bottle necks caught between my knuckles

as I delivered a dozen, six in each arm,
or carried a case of twenty-four on my back,
tin can shacks selling them out of the icebox;

maybe take breaks by the beach, sleep shirtless
under a palm tree, my hat covering my face,
or see the country from the bed of the truck,
road cutting across the mountains, overlooking the sea.

At night, I always wanted to join day laborers,
drink seriously, blow out a clatter of laughs.

Instead my hair is dusted in chalk,
my throat dried from shouting all day into the air.

Sometimes when I can't stand it, I drive along the Pacific,
think about the man I wanted to be, highway stretching
across the state, crops unrolling along the side.

I'm three countries away from that wagon

grinding its chains down the road, a nest of huts—plaited cane
and mud—where two men were shot in front of me,
went down like a sack of rice. They were twins.

I lost the sun no longer thickening over the roof of the house,
the man who could drive across the country,

unload case after case to the neighborhoods,
but I know how to pull a book off the shelf,
place it under the yellow circle of light,

see the fallen bodies, the dirt rags
of clay and blood, those that keep saying I'm alive.

On first listening to Coltrane

I loved him, full-body wail of a tenor, large and round,
his crooked fingers on brass, choking the hollow horn
with God caught in his throat, the way he pushed

a mountain into his saxophone, it hit me
like a hundred iron wheels steamed down
the tracks, coal-driven, rolling solid

through the tongue of night, darker
than tar, grinding thoughts into sounds,

gush of phrases that spiral forward,
climb the tip of the wave about to uncurl,
spiral back, plunge and collapse

into this note, blessed and obsessed, perfect

in the palm of my hand, touched by the earth,
wet and small, dust and bones, the heavy weight of corn,

the wind that comes wrapped in fish and salt,
the cry of the crow high above the road

where he stands spindly as a tree,
the cymbal splash of sunlight, the horn blaring;
you'd think he's cracking a branch

hooked in the river, green and growing, leaves carried
with the current, twirling, black and swollen,

bobbing along the line he plays,

plays again, until the branch finally snaps,
the driftwood swelling along the bank,
waves reflecting the bed of rock,

and then rain—the falling pins of rain—
the river that runs to the shore.

Pilgrimage

When the L.A. river rolls
rapidly along the freeways,
torn, thrashing waves
slapping against concrete,

cold echo of the wind
moving among trees,
I'll walk back to Sonsonate.
When the late sun leaves

palm trees sound asleep,
ragged dusty branches
without fruit or shade,
or the full throat of a bird,

I'll take off my shoes
and walk back to Sonsonate.
The night I hang these shoes
over telephone wires,

swinging to the clank,
pop, stop and go;
rhythms and moans
of the traffic, I'll walk back.

I'll walk back when the moon
drops into Echo Park Lake,
pale fingered dime
making a sloppish sound,

long blades of grass
rising out of freeway cracks.
By the time the fall of the rain
breaks into the streets, washes

the gray film of smoke,
all the gasoline of the night
down the gutter, I'll take off my hat,
walk back to Sonsonate.

When the city falls
at my feet, its architecture
collapsing to its knees,
weight of cars cooling

in the heat, I'll pack my bones,
head back to Sonsonate,
down a road of coffee beans,
old broken-down guitars.

Small Country

A match light in the cupped hands of a soldier,
that's my country, which never answers my letters,
never writes about hospitals gasping for breath,

the wounded child who still hears a cricket
singing below his bed. I fall, rise again
somewhere downtown, stepping over puddles,

those in rags called "nobodies." I know
how to disappear like a body in a plastic bag
by a green lake. I know how to roll

down a ravine, wait all night after a small war
for telegrams that never reach your door.
I know how to follow great avenues,

the stump of a cigarette between my teeth unlit.
I've wasted so many postcards, so many letters
remembering a spot, mid-continent—all its dead:

the decapitated ones, the blue ones, those known
as bodies in the morning papers, names printed in black,
so many words searching broken spears

of cornfields, bones later fossilized in the earth.
How many dawns shall I talk with the dead,
writing precisely, in three lines without meter, the death

of a boy or girl, all those coffins carried
into the daylight street? I want the rain to drop
like rocks, plow through rows of corn

before they come to a close, wash the land twisted,
rooted in bones, mud that clings to our shoes;
women and men of clay drenched in a storm.

I want to fold the city like a dark blanket,
throw it over my shoulder and rest.
I'm tired of the dirt, their white open mouths.

After Ashes

I

For my immigrant father, driven mad by the L.A. heat,
his hands a collection of slits,
creases from pulling weeds, dusty road long and black
unrolling his way back home, his swollen yellow knees,

the locust wind speaking broken sentences
to the cornfields bending
with the wind, red sun buried
behind the mountains,

where the dead weight of men carries
rifles and rags, hears the rattle of their guns,
bullets in their chests that blot out the sun,
their knees collapse to the ground
as cows break their snouts on the grass.

For my uncle, who drinks himself
to the bottoms of bottles: gin and tonic,
vodka, lemon or lime, his hand
curled around the glass, stumbles into streets

blue with cold, all the wheels and gears
busted into pieces, cars that jolt and stop,
exhale the water—heat of oil and gas,

trees that bend to the side, buses he rides,
their breath of smoke, factory stacks
that rise into gray skies.

For my mother, elbowing her way
through the crowd, her purse tucked under her arm,

a bag of groceries propped against the wall
as she opens the door, words stuck
on the tip of her tongue, looking for a phrase,
a line that can crop
the lilacs down, translate

                    the ribcage of her country.

II

For Father Martínez, who barks the Sunday sermon
on the white belly of God, tortured Christ
slumped on his back—the pull
and slow drag of the body across the city
—eyes like dead fish, dry yellow mouth.

For the Mission boys, who kick it nice
and slow in the corner, cursing and laughing,
cops in their black-and-whites,
pinning a boy to the hood of a car,
batons flashing in the light;

their fathers, working men,
who plaster domes, raise walls of bricks,
their rough fingers among the rubble of concrete,
fallen metal beams, their backs growing old,
yellow and cold, their breath,
a faint hammer-beat;

the bird flying in a film of smog,
descending with brown wings, pulling
toward the curve, broken bottles, stained floors.
No sunflower cloud or river song;

For the piles of rubble
and curling smoke, burning engines,
splintered wings that remain caught in our throats.
They are the early cold slap of winter, that icy steel
of barbed wire that wraps around your coat,

cuts your face, leaves you stoned. We're nothing
but a grain in the street, nothing next to a piece of brick.

III

For this earth, cold, dark earth, this earth that rolls
below our feet, this flat circle of earth barren with rocks,
deep roots grasping about the bones, blue mountains that rise
and fall like whales, one after the other, their backs smooth,
bending against the sky, wind that spreads over the ocean,
gallops, waves mounting, rolling onto the shore,
throbbing with fish, striped and plump, racing in the water,

                      crooked fingers of the sea.

What is it that makes the sun slop into the sea,
the moon plunge deep into the land?

Open the earth, this cemented earth
filled with rubble, grasping for breath.

Dig a hole, deep beyond the gravel
and return to the blackened earth, moist, forked with roots.

No movement or sound, everything a complete stop,
so I can stand upon a hill, see the line of the ocean,
the sky arching above me,
                      scuffle the earth.

IV

This is exactly where I want to be,

where the wind blows against the house,
metal pipes between walls that cough
and groan, faint whistle of a train
that pulls across the city.

It's here between the opening and closing
mouth of night that I write

the remaining walls of a church,

the broken calligraphy of the arc
collapsed, buried in smoke.

It's here among the burial mounds of black ash
that I write a word, a sentence, scratch it out

till I see a country so small
your index finger can cover it on a school map,
all the bodies dumped and slumped
in the swamp of a ravine, those cooped
in a dark grave of roots and rocks.
                              They're mine,

the women and men who wear the same shoes,
gather the same words, learn the alphabet
like a simple mathematical calculation,
                    give them back
before they raise sticks and stones,
before I am old and no longer here.

IV

The Art of Exile

On the Pan American Highway, somewhere
between the north and south continent,
you come across a chain of volcanoes,

a coast with a thick growth of palm trees,
crunching waves of the sea; an isthmus
Neruda called "slender earth like a whip."

When the road bends, turns into a street,
the walls splattered with "Yanqui Go Home!!!"
you see a boy fifteen years old,

barefoot, sniffing glue in a small plastic bag.
An old woman in an apron will step out,
say, "This is the right street."

In the public square, there will be no friend
from school to welcome you, no drive
to Sonsonate, city of coconuts,

no one to order cold Pilseners, oyster
cocktails, or convince the waitress
into dancing a cumbia or two with you.

Instead, at the local bar, you'll raise
a bottle next to strangers, stub
your cigarette out on the floor.

You'll watch a country ten years
after the civil war: an old man sitting
on the curb, head between knees,

open hand stretched out.
Everything will hurt, your hair,
your toenails, even your shoes.

You'll curse dusty streets, demented
sun slowly burning the nape of your neck,
stray dogs following you to the park.

By nightfall, you drag yourself back to the bars,
looking for a lost country in a shot of Tíc Táck.
Against the wall, three men with their guitars.

When you lie on a hotel bed,
too tired to sleep, when you feel torn,
twisted like an old newspaper, blown

from city to city, you have reached the place.
You have begun to speak like a man
by the side of the road, barefoot.

Rattle

I like the tobacco smell of them,
coffee-stained wood in my hands,
two cannonballs a conquistador shot
into the coast of Cuzcatlán.

Two dried gourds with dead seeds,
not the colorful maracas from Cuba,
those mambo coconuts, but two stones
roughly carved into black orchids,

below the stems, a shantytown
by the foot of a volcano,
Nahuizalco, 1932:
cobblestone streets, a white shell church.

Peasants, thumbs tied together behind their backs,
fall into trenches like doors fall to the ground.
Two black craters, two open mouths,
gravel and ash in my hands.

Roque

Nothing has changed since you left.
Cornfields still flash like daggers.
Stars are nail heads hammered
against the sky. "Roque," over

and over again, unraveling the rolling "r"
on my tongue, I'll say it. I'll pick it,
pluck your words about women,
men running through a rain of dead birds.

> *the forever undocumented . . .*
> *the first ones to pull a knife . . .*

Roque, I'm waiting for you to come home
cursing like a circus clown in times of war
or a grave digger ready to bury his bones,
roam the streets like a skinny dog.

Even the cops are afraid to walk at dawn.
They stay behind bars, weave tales
of how the government fell flat
the night you faced the firing squad,

then fled to Cuba, reappeared
in Niña Concha's bar, washing down
the best black oysters in town.
Policemen found you, beer in hand;

your wrists clasped, once again in jail.
This time, an earthquake cracked
the prison walls open, and like a moon
free from a cloud, you slipped into dusk.

You didn't believe in God, but guards
swear on their mothers you prayed
as if you were back with the Jesuits.
Some say it's all a myth. Others say

you left for Prague, always writing
about your country, small as a paper cut,
that tiny republic tattooed on your body,
its women, men dumped by the roadside.

Somewhere, your grave remains unmarked.
The earth remembers your name, soiled and wet.
Rocks know your smell of leaf mold.
Let each root drain you of blood,

let this crag be your tombstone, these weeds
your lilacs growing tall, these branches—dried
and weathered—your garland, and death:
this cold, naked moon you shot against the sky.

Two-bass lines

for Charles Mingus

He sees himself leaving his body,
seventeen again, fingers plucking strings,

picking feathers off a dead bird,
tearing roots out of the earth, or peeling

an orange rind in a single stroke. Sometimes
it's a strand of hair caught in the corner

of a woman's mouth, the slow pull and graze
of the bow. He sees the boy

bowlegged, pigeon-toed, hair combed and greased,
index and middle fingers taped together,

closer to Watts, dirt streets that rain turned to mud,
the crackly broadcast of big bands,

always disappearing, closer to his bass
standing in the acoustics of a church.

He's carried out of his New York apartment
like a clown who gets hit

with a five-pound sack of flour
and the crowd rolls on the floor laughing—

circus waltz in the background. Two officers
in black clasp his arms, his eyes

two small dimes, fat slap of meat hanging
over the belt, piano slammed

against the rumble of trucks. The city falls on him
in the backseat of a black and white car.

Bicycle

When I was ten, I rode these blue mountains
with no hands, down these streets, out of alleys,

backstreets curving into a road, trucks raising dust,
grasshoppers green and golden in the turf,

beyond the coffee field, a clearing and a stream—
clear gutter of water—and then the hill,
the mountain that never ends.

Now, a tree, black and charred, spikes up
like a claw rising out of the earth.

The brown waters drag among weeds.
Tin cans, rusted pipes.

No sea of grass.

I've returned to ruins, brick houses
crusted with dust, tin flats piled high

above cliffs, small settlements
of bamboo and mud,
                              buses black
hissing their greasy tongues, the broken
backs of cows lost in the garbage dump.

This was home,
where I saw the terrible eye of the trout,
slick belly wide open in the hand of a merchant,

rows of fish wrapped in newspaper,
stacked against the crushed ice.

The men were reduced to clay, year
after year of digging graves, sinking spades

deep in the earth, lowering
bodies cold and flat, boxed in coffins.

Those nights in my sleep, I watched fingers
search through the loam, pulling deep roots
and worms out of the earth.

A woman unraveled out of her open legs
a child ball.
              I come to my house,
small and silent, green from the rain,
overgrown trees and pigweed, door
red with rust.
              I've returned to a child
in the doorway, sandals and shorts,
belly swollen with milk and flies.

A wheel, its broken spokes
stick out of the mud.

Bury This Pig

Behind the cornfield, we scaled the mountainside
     looking for a foothold among the crags,

rooting out weeds, trampling on trash,
     the trek as if it were a holy crusade:

bodies armored, mounted on horses,
     banners fluttering in the air.

Then one morning, we stumbled upon the thing,
     dead, cramped in a ditch, covered in ants,

trotters grimy, a purple snout of flies
     and not a dollop of blood,

but a thick piece of hide, cradling
     about fifty pounds of hog.

Someone said, "Kush! Kush!"
     as if to awaken the thing.

I thought about the carcass, blood-slick,
     staggering into the room,

grumbling and drowning as if deep in the mud,
     eyes buckled in fear,

bones breaking down to the ground, open
     to the chop and tear of human hands:

pork and lard, forefeet, fatback cut into slabs,
     an organ fattened and butchered.

It continued for weeks, a few of us
        meeting in the afternoons

just to look at the steaming belly, maggots
        stealing the gray of the brain,

each time, one more barefoot boy
        probing the eye socket with a stick.

Some of us came back armed
        with picks and bars, shovels dusty in our hands,

until the ground groaned with war.
        The sky fell and cracked the earth.

How was I to know
        they would be hooked, hacked,

snouts smashed on the wall,
        their bodies corkscrews on the floor?

How was I to know
        I would bury this pig, rock after rock?

Tunnel

I'm left behind following their footsteps, wandering
through an old ruin, my insect wings taking me to hospitals

where I ask the doctor, "Have you seen these men?"
He offers the emergency room, where death sniffs like a lonesome dog.

I enter the stone church, question the priest.
All he knows is the groan of the Pope. I ramble in and out of prisons,

deciphering photos, black and white, asking for peasants
that come from clay, another body banished from the skin of the land.

I search for boats across the stuttering waves of the sea,
buses cutting across the borderline. When I ask for names,

they're already gone, full throttle along the roll of the road.
I walk streets of gasoline and tar, houses gutted, doors and knobs,

peeking through windows like a soldier who returns after the war,
looking at portraits on walls, dining tables, desolate chairs,

the flaming flowers of sulfur that take me to the one-room
railroad apartment, back to the stones piled by the road, the riverside

woman who bangs clothes against the boulders,
says, "No matter where they go, they will always be

a broken branch from the trunk of a tree, a leaf's odyssey."
I flounder through patches of dirt like a grave digger with shovel

ready to open the ground, cut a gash along the black earth,
see the water creep out into the air.

Acknowledgments

To the editors of the following journals and anthologies in which some of
these poems or earlier versions (some under slightly different titles) first
appeared, I extend grateful acknowledgment.

AGNI: "Bury This Pig"

Blue Mesa Review: "Roque"

Bilingual Review: "Immigration Blues, 1980," "Latest News," "Whitman"

Crab Orchard Review: "The Art of Exile"

The Georgia Review: "The decade the country became known throughout
the world"

Hanging Loose Press: "Guayaberas"

The Los Angeles Review: "Whitman"

North American Review: "This is for Henry"

Notre Dame Review: "Pilgrimage"

Obsidian III: "At Minton's"

Palabra: "By the Highway," "Two o'clock in the morning," "Self-Portrait
with Crow"

Portland Review: "Radio," "A Dying Sun"

Poetry International: "1978"

Puerto Del Sol: "This Earth"

Rattle: "Duke Ellington, Santa Ana, El Salvador, 1974"

The Sow's Ear Poetry Review: "Rattle"

Terra Incognita: "Late December," "Foreign Language"

"Bird" was included in *Birds in the Hand*, North Point Press (2003), edited
by Dylan Nelson and Kent Nelson. "This is for Henry" was included
in *Blue Arc West: An Anthology of California Poets*, Tebot Bach (2006),
edited by Paul Suntup, Dima Hilal & Mindy Nettifee.

"This Earth" received the Fourth Annual Prentice Hall Writing Contest
award. "Drinking Beer in East L.A." was selected by Writers at Work for
its postcard publication project, distributed for free throughout the city
and funded by the City of Los Angeles Cultural Affairs Department.

Special thanks to Suzanne Lummis, Francisco Aragón, Virgil Suárez, Dorianne Laux, Joe Millar, Pimone Triplett, Garrett Hongo and Yusef Komunyakaa. In deep gratitude to Margarita Alfaro, Rolando Archila, Arnoldo Archila and Mario De La Fuente. This collection of poems would not be possible without the care and support of my beautiful wife Lory Bedikian. In memory of Chocha.

William Archila was born in Santa Ana, El Salvador, in 1968. When he was only twelve, he and his family immigrated to the United States to escape the civil war that was tearing his country apart. He eventually became an English teacher and earned his MFA in poetry from the University of Oregon. His poems have appeared in *Agni, Blue Mesa Review, Crab Orchard Review, The Georgia Review, The Los Angeles Review, Notre Dame Review, Poetry International, and Puerto del Sol,* among others. He lives in Los Angeles with his wife. *The Art of Exile* is his first book.